# Foreword

America has the most diverse collection of names in the world. The next time you pick up your phone book, flip through the pages and ask yourself where all those people who settled in your neighborhood came from originally. Every name, every face, reveals a piece of the puzzle. Most of our parents, grandparents or great grandparents came here from another country. America is a nation of immigrants.

In this book, people of all ages, who arrived between 1890 and 1910, tell their stories. It is a fascinating part of our history.

In our efforts to understand the people who make up the citizens of our nation, we are lucky to have so many personal diaries, interviews, photos, songs, and letters from those years. We call these documents "primary sources" because they were recorded at the time or later by immigrants themselves. When you read the primary sources in this book, you will get a feeling of what it was like to come to America one hundred years ago. Remember, though, that each person had his or her own special experience.

Most of these immigrants started out from Southern or Eastern Europe. The majority went through the immigration offices at Ellis Island in New York Harbor. Historians write books about this wave of immigration. These are called "secondary sources" because they are not first-hand

reports or eye-witness accounts. Secondary sources are useful as they give a larger picture of the times.

In 1890, conditions seemed hopeless for many Europeans. No matter how hard they worked, things did not get better in the daily course of their lives. When these people heard that America offered everyone the opportunity to better themselves by jobs and education, many decided start a new life in this "golden land."

It is never easy to leave your home, your friends, community and country—forever. Life was sometimes harder than the new Americans had expected. Unfortunately, they were not always made welcome. However, most of the million or so a year who came here around the turn of the twentieth century found peace, freedom, the opportunity to earn a living, and hope. In turn, they brought determination, creativity, and the great diversity which makes America today.

Today, immigrants continue to arrive in America. Listen as they share their stories. America's heritage is a mixture of cultures which developed on this land or were brought by those who came here for a new life.

# Excerpts from *Of Thee We Sing: Immigrants and American History, by Dale Steiner*

All Americans are either immigrants themselves or the descendants of immigrants. There are no exceptions. Even the Indians, despite being called "native Americans," are not as a people truly indigenous to America. Their distant ancestors were immigrants who crossed a now-vanished land bridge from Siberia to Alaska during the most recent ice age, 10,000 to 40,000 years ago. There are, of course, several differences which separate these first Americans from those to whom we customarily attach the label "immigrant." The time of their arrival is perhaps the most obvious of these. The fact that all later immigrants were required, in some way, to adjust to a host society while the Indians did not, also sets the first Americans apart...the Indians were not really aware that they were immigrating—they were entirely ignorant of their ultimate destination.

But they were nonetheless immigrants. And because all Americans are immigrants, or descended from immigrants, the study of immigration is an integral part of any inquiry into American history. Immigration has been a continuous and constant factor in America's economic growth, political change and cultural development. It is not something which can properly be compartmentalized...in a single chapter of a book which purports to survey American history. Yet that is precisely how the subject is handled in almost every instance....

This approach distorts our undestanding of American history. It obscures the nature of colonial society, for example, by referring to "colonists" and "indentured servants" without acknowledging that the settlers of Jamestown, the Pilgrims of Plymouth Plantation, and the Puritan founders of Massachusetts were in fact immigrants...Likewise, it would be foolish to examine slavery without at the same time attempting some analysis of Africans as immigrants—that is, the slave trade.

...American blacks are often portrayed as outsiders engaged in a constant struggle to achieve a place in the social mainstream. Yet in terms of how deeply their roots extend into our nation's soil, they are more "American" than are most of their white countrymen. The great majority of black Americans are descended from Africans who were brought to America prior to the prohibition of the slave trade in 1808. Most white Americans, on the other hand, trace their ancestry to Europeans who came to the United States between 1815 and 1914, when immigration swelled to a flood tide....The slave system aimed consciously at the suppression of their past as a means of discouraging organization and forestalling rebellion. One result of this was the creation of a culture among slaves that was a uniquely American amalgamation of many African peoples. In contrast, other immigrants often clung desperately to their past in an effort to cushion the shock of exposure to a new way of life.... Although America is a nation of immigrants, it has exhibited throughout its history a strong undercurrent of suspicion toward them. New arrivals have frequently been held at arm's length by more established Americans—overlooked, despised, rejected. At the same time, however, those immigrants were being woven into the nation's social fabric. To examine their experience is to study the evolution of American society, but from the vantage point of its underside.

In order for immigrants to come to America, they had to depart from somewhere else. In other words, immigrants are emigrants. These two words, similar in appearance and in meaning, in fact describe the same social and historical process, but from different perspectives, the *immigrant* migrates into a country, the *emigrant* leaves his homeland for some other place.

Perhaps the most effective way to arrive at the meaning of that tremendous movement of humanity to America is to consider its participants as emigrants: to attempt to understand where they came from, why they left home, what they sought. Only then can we begin to evaluate and appreciate where they settled, how they were received, what they found.

*Emigrants on board a crowded ship bound for the United States*

...Emigration represented an almost violent act of separation from everything that people knew or held dear—family, friends, home, culture, landscape. It was, in most cases, a tremendous sacrifice, producing enormous trauma. To choose to leave home, even for the vague promise of America, was by no means a painless decision....

...And immigration was almost invariably an excursion into the unknown. Recognition of that fact in turn makes it clear that the "typical" immigrant was not typical at all, but was instead—

by definition—a rather exceptional person. For us to extract full value from whatever lessons their experiences may afford us, it is essential that we not lose sight of the fact that immigrants who came to America from other societies were extraordinary people....

People are curious about other people; they are interested in learning the details of other lives. That holds true not only for the present, but for the past as well. Viewing history through the lens of an individual's life brings clarity and focus to the events which occurred during that lifetime. Biography enlivens history; it personalizes the abstract and animates the boring. And it reminds us that history is, after all, nothing more nor less than the record of the aggregate of humanity—that history is people.

# The Statue of Liberty

*A gift of friendship from France, the Statue of Liberty was erected in New York Harbor in 1886 and became a symbol of welcome for millions of immigrants. Engraved on a tablet is a poem by Emma Lazarus:*

> "Keep, ancient lands, your storied pomp!" cries she
> With silent lips. "Give me your tired, your poor,
> Your huddled masses yearning to breathe free;
> The wretched refuse of your teeming shore,
> Send these, the homeless, tempest-test to me.
> I lift my lamp beside the golden door!"

*Emma was the daughter of an old Spanish family in New York. At first she did not know or care about the history of her people. She wrote delicate poems about Greek myths.*

*Once, while looking at Greek statues in a museum, she was introduced to an Englishman. He asked why she preferred the Greeks to her own Jewish people, who were suffering terribly in Europe.*

*On the way home, a newsboy shouted, "Pogroms in Russia! Read about the pogroms against the Jews!" She bought a paper, and that night Emma Lazarus began writing strong and beautiful poetry about the persecution of her people, which had been going on since the twelfth century in Europe. After writing of the pogroms in 1881 she worked with refugees in America and composed the poem which you can still see on the Statue of Liberty, today.*

*Liberty enlightening the world, Frédéric Auguste Bartholdi, c. 1884*

# Excerpts from Mary Antin's Diary, 1893

*Mary Antin was one of thousands of Russian Jews who fled from persecution. Her journal was her own day-to-day account, in Yiddish, written as she immigrated to America at age eleven. Later she included it in her autobiography,* The Promised Land.

...Driven by a necessity for bettering the family circumstances, and by certain minor forces which cannot now be named, my father began to think seriously of casting his lot with the great stream of emigrants. Many family councils were held before it was agreed that the plan must be carried out. Then came the parting; for it was impossible for the whole family to go at once. I remember it, though I was only eight. It struck me as rather interesting to stand on the platform before the train, with a crowd of friends weeping in sympathy with us, and father waving his hat for our special benefit, and saying—the last words we heard him speak as the train moved off—

"Good-bye, Plotzk, forever!"

Then followed three long years of hope and doubt for father in America and us in Russia. There were toil and suffering and waiting and anxiety for all. There were—but to tell of all that happened in those years I should have to write a separate history. The happy day came when we received the long-coveted summons. And what stirring times followed! The period of preparation was one of constant delight to us children. We were four—my two sisters, one brother and myself. Our playmates looked up to us in respectful admiration; neighbors, if they made no direct investigations, bribed us with nice things for information as to what was going into every box, package and basket. And the house was dismantled—people came and carried off the furniture; closets, sheds and other nooks were emptied of their contents; the great wood-pile was taken away until only a few logs remained; ancient treasures such as women are so loathe to part with, and which mother had carried with her from a dear little house whence poverty had driven us, were brought to light from their hiding places, and sacrificed at the altar whose flames were consuming so much that was fraught with precious association and endeared by family tradition; the number of bundles and boxes increased daily, and our home vanished hourly; the rooms became quite uninhabitable, at last, and we children glanced in glee, to the anger of the echoes, when we heard that in the evening we were to start upon our journey....

At this time, cholera was raging in Russia, and was spread by emigrants going to America in the countries through which they travelled. To stop this danger, measures were taken to make emigration from Russia more difficult than ever. I believe that at all times the crossing of the boundary between Russia and Germany was a source of trouble to Russians, but with a special passport this was easily overcome. When, however, the traveller could not afford to supply himself with one, the boundary was crossed by stealth, and many amusing anecdotes are told of persons who crossed in some disguise, often that of a mujik who said he was going to the town on the German side to sell some goods, carried for the purpose of ensuring the success of the ruse. When several such tricks had been played on the guards it became very risky,...

The doctor asked many questions about our health, and of what nationality we were. Then he asked about various things, as where we were going to, if we had tickets, how much money we had, where we came from, to whom we were going, etc., etc., making a note of every answer he received. This done, he shook his head with his shining helmet on it, and said slowly (I imagined he enjoyed frightening us), "With these third class tickets you cannot go to America now, because it is forbidden to admit emigrants into Germany who have not at least second class tickets. You will have to return to Russia unless you pay at the office here to have your tickets changed for second class ones." After a few minutes' calculation and reference to the notes he had made, he added calmly, "I find you will need two hundred rubles to get your tickets exchanged;" and, as the finishing stroke to his pleasing communications, added, "Your passports are of no use at all now because the necessary part has to be torn out, whether you are allowed to pass or not." A plain, short speech he made of it, that cruel man. Yet every word sounded in our ears with an awful sound that stopped the beating of our

*Eastern Europeans emigrants on board ship, 1899*

17

hearts for a while—sounded like the ringing of funeral bells to us, and yet without the mournfully sweet music those bells make, that they might heal while they hurt.

We were homeless, houseless, and friendless in a strange place. We had hardly money enough to last us through the voyage for which we had hoped and waited for three long years. We had suffered much that the reunion we longed for might come about; we had prepared ourselves to suffer more in order to bring it about, and had parted with those we loved, with places that were dear to us in spite of what we passed through in them, never again to see them, as were convinced—all for the same dear end. With strong hopes and high spirits that hid the sad parting, we had started on our long journey. And now we were checked so unexpectedly but surely, the blow coming from where we little expected it, being as we believed, safe in that quarter. And that is why the simple words had such a frightful meaning to us. We had received a wound we knew not how to heal.

When mother had recovered enough to speak she began to argue with the gendarme, telling him our story and begging him to be kind. The children were frightened by what they understood, and all but cried. I was only wondering what would happen, and wishing I could pour out my grief in tears, as the others did; but when I feel deeply I seldom show it in that way, and always wish I could.

Mother's supplications, and perhaps the children's indirect ones, had more effect than I supposed they would. The officer was moved, even if he had just said that tears would not be accepted instead of money, and gave us such kind advice that I began to be sorry I had thought him cruel, for it was easy to see that he was only doing his duty and had no part in our trouble that he could be blamed for, now that I had more kindly thoughts of him.

He said that we would now be taken to Keebart, a few versts' distance from Verzbolovo, where one Herr Schidorsky lived. This man, he said, was well known for miles around, and we were to tell him our story and ask him to help us, which he probably would, being very kind....

Towards evening we came into Berlin....

This was another scene of bewildering confusion, parents losing their children, and little ones crying; baggage being thrown together in one corner of the yard, heedless of contents, which suffered in consequence; those white-clad Germans shouting commands always accompanied with "Quick! Quick!"; the confused passengers obeying all orders like meek children, only questioning now and then what was going to be done with them.

And no wonder if in some minds stories arose of people being captured by robbers, murderers, and the like. Here we had been taken to a lonely place where only that house was to be seen; our things were taken away, our friends separated from us; a man came to inspect us, as if to ascertain our full value; strange looking people driving us about like dumb animals, helpless and unresisting; children we could not see, crying in a way that suggested terrible things; ourselves driven into a little room where a great kettle was boiling on a little stove; our clothes taken off, our bodies rubbed with a slippery substance that might be any bad thing; a shower of warm water let down on us without warning; again driven to another little room where we sit, wrapped in woollen blankets till large, coarse bags are brought in, their contents turned out and we see only a cloud of steam, and hear the women's orders to dress ourselves, quick, quick, or else we'll miss—something we cannot hear. We are forced to pick out our clothes from among all the others, with the steam blinding us; we choke, cough, entreat the women to give us time; they persist, "Quick, quick, or you'll miss the train!" Oh, so we really won't be murdered! They are only making us ready for the continuing of our journey, cleaning us of all suspicions of dangerous germs. Thank God!...

The horses never weary. Still they run. There are no houses now in view, save now and then a solitary one, far away. I can see the ocean. Oh, it is stormy. The dark waves roll inward, the white foam flies high in the air; deep sounds come from it. The wheels and hoofs make a great noise; the wind is stronger, and says, "Do you hear the sea?" And the ocean's roar threatens. The sea threatens, and the wind bids me hear it, and the hoofs and the wheels repeat the command, and so do the trees, by gestures.

Yes, we are frightened. We are very still. Some Polish women over there have fallen asleep, and the rest of us look such a picture of woe, and yet so funny, it is a sight to see and remember.

At last, at last! Those unwearied horses have stopped. Where? In front of a brick building, the only one on a large, broad street, where only the trees, and, in the distance, the passing trains can be seen. Nothing else. The ocean, too, is shut out....

As usual, many questions were asked, the new ones being about our tickets. Then each person, children included, had to pay three marcs—one for the wagon that brought us over and two for food and lodgings, till our various ships should take us away....

When the doctor was through with us he told us to go to Number Five. Now wasn't that like in a prison? We walked up and down a long yard looking, among a row of low, numbered doors, for ours, when we heard an exclamation of, "Oh, Esther! how do you happen to be here?" and, on seeing the speaker, found it to be an old friend of ours from Plotzk. She had gone long before us, but her ship hadn't arrived yet. She was surprised to see us because we had no intention of going when she went....

Our friend explained that Number Five was only for Jewish women and girls, and the beds were sleeping rooms, dining rooms, parlors, and everything else, kitchens excepted. It seemed so, for some were lounging on the beds, some sitting up, some otherwise engaged, and all were talking and laughing and making a great noise. Poor things! there was nothing else to do in that prison....

The greatest event was the arrival of some ship to take some of the waiting passengers. When the gates were opened and the lucky ones said good bye, those left behind felt hopeless of ever seeing the gates open for them. It was both pleasant and painful, for the strangers grew to be fast friends in a day and really rejoiced in each other's fortune, but the regretful envy could not be helped either.

Amid such events as these a day was like a month at least. Eight of these we had spent in quarantine when a great commotion was noticed among the people of Number Five and those of the corresponding number in the men's division. There was good reason for it. You remember that it was April and Passover was coming on; in fact, it began that night. The great question was, Would we be able to keep it exactly according to the host of rules to be obeyed? You who know all about the great holiday can understand what the answer to that question meant to us. Think of all the work and care and money it takes to supply a family with all the things proper and necessary, and you will see that to supply a few hundred was no small matter. Now, were they going to take care that all was perfectly right, and could we trust them if they promised, or should we be forced to break any of the laws that ruled the holiday?

All day long there was talking and questioning and debating and threatening that "we would rather starve than touch anything we were not sure of." And we meant it. So some men and women went to the overseer to let him know what he had to look out for. He assured them that he would rather starve along with us than allow anything to be in the least wrong. Still, there was more discussing and shaking of heads, for they were not sure yet.

There was not a crumb anywhere to be found, because what bread we received was too precious for any of it to be wasted; but the women made a great show of cleaning up Number Five, while they sighed and looked sad and told one another of the good hard times they had at home getting ready for Passover. Really, hard as it is, when one is used to it from childhood, it seems part of the holiday, and can't be left out. To sit down and wait for supper as on other nights seemed like breaking one of the laws. So they tried hard to be busy.

At night we were called by the overseer (who tried to look more important than ever in his holiday clothes—not his best, though) to the feast spread in one of the unoccupied rooms. We were ready for it, and anxious enough. We had had neither bread nor matzo for dinner, and were more hungry than ever, if that is possible. We now found everything really prepared; there were the pillows covered with a snow-white spread, new oil-cloth on the newly scrubbed tables, some little candles stuck in a basin of sand on the window-sill for the women, and—a sure sign of a holiday—both gas lamps burning. Only one was used on other nights.

Happy to see these things, and smell the supper, we took our places and waited. Soon the cook came in and filled some glasses with wine from two bottles,—one yellow, one red. Then she gave to each person—exactly one and a half matzos; also some cold meat, burned almost to a coal for the occasion.

The young man—bless him—who had the honor to perform the ceremonies, was, fortunately for us all, one of the passengers. He felt for and with us, and it happened—just a coincidence—that the greater part of the ceremony escaped from his book as he turned the leaves. Though strictly religious, nobody felt in the least guilty about it, especially on account of the wine; for, when we came to the place where you have to drink the wine, we found it tasted like good vinegar, which made us all choke and gasp, and one little girl screamed "Poison!" so that all laughed, and the leader, who tried to go on, broke down too at the sight of the wry faces he saw; while the overseer looked shocked, the cook nearly set her gown on fire by overthrowing the candles with her apron (used to hide her face) and all wished our Master Overseer had to drink that "wine" all his days.

Think of the same ceremony as it is at home, then of this one just described. Do they even resemble each other?

Well, the leader got through amid much giggling and sly looks among the girls who understood the trick, and frowns of the older people (who secretly blessed him for it). Then, half hungry, all went to bed and dreamed of food in plenty.

No other dreams? Rather! For the day that brought the Passover brought us—our own family—the most glorious news: our ship had arrived to carry us from Hamburg to Boston and my father!...

For sixteen days the ship was our world....Oh, what solemn thoughts I had! How deeply I felt the greatness, the power of the scene! The immeasurable distance from horizon to horizon; the huge billows forever changing their shapes—now only a wavy and rolling plain, now a chain of great mountains, coming and going farther away;...and the deep, solemn groans of the sea, sounding as if all the voices of the world had been turned into sighs and then gathered into that one mournful sound—so deeply did I feel the presence of these things, that the feeling became one of awe, both painful and sweet, and stirring and warming, and deep and calm and grand.

I would imagine myself all alone on the ocean, and Robinson Crusoe was very real to me. I was alone sometimes. I was aware of no human presence; I was conscious only of sea and sky and something I did not understand.

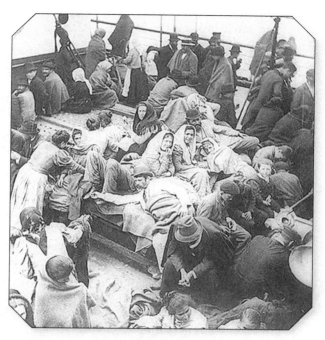

*Emigrants sailing to Ellis Island*

And as I listened to its solemn voice, I felt as if I had found a friend, and knew that I loved the ocean. It seemed as if it were within as well as without, part of myself; and I wondered how I had lived without it, and if I could ever part with it...

The morning was glorious. It was the eighth of May, the seventeenth day after we left Hamburg. The sky was clear and blue, the sun shone brightly, as if to congratulate us that we had safely crossed the stormy sea, and to apologize for having kept away from us so long. The sea had lost its fury; it was almost as quiet as it had been at Hamburg before we started, and its color was a beautiful greenish blue. Birds were all the time in the air, and it was worth while [sic] to live merely to hear their songs. And soon, oh joyful sight! we saw the tops of two trees!...

Oh, what a beautiful scene! No corner of the earth is half so fair as the lovely picture before us. It came to view suddenly,—a green field, a real field with grass on it, and large houses, and the dearest hens and little chickens in all the world, and trees, and birds, and people at work....

Before the ship had fully stopped, the climax of our joy was reached. One of us espied the figure and face we had longed to see for three long years. In a moment five passengers on the "Polynesia" were crying, "Papa," and gesticulating, and laughing, and hugging one another, and going wild together....

Oh, dear! Why can't we get off the hateful ship? Why can't papa come to us? Why so many ceremonies at the landing?...

Now imagine yourself parting with all you love, believing it to be a parting for life; breaking up your home, selling the things that years have made dear to you; starting

*Immigrants arriving at Ellis Island, 1907*

on a journey without the least experience in travelling, in the face of many inconveniences on account of the want of sufficient money; being met with disappointment where it was not to be expected; with rough treatment everywhere, till you are forced to go and make friends for yourself among strangers; being obliged to sell some of your most necessary things to pay bills you did not willingly incur; being mistrusted and searched, then half starved, and lodged in common with a multitude of strangers; suffering the miseries of seasickness, the disturbances and alarms of a stormy sea for sixteen days; and then stand within, a few yards of him for whom you did all this, unable to even speak to him easily. How do you feel?

Oh, it's our turn at last! We are questioned, examined, and dismissed! A rush over the planks on one side, over the ground on the other, six wild beings cling to each other, bound by a common bond of tender joy, and the long parting is at an END.

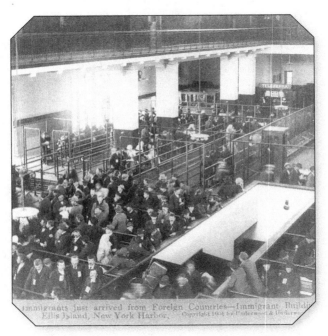

Immigrants just arrived from Foreign Countries—Immigrant Building Ellis Island, New York Harbor. Copyright 1904 by Underwood & Underwood

*Newly arrived immigrants in the waiting hall at Ellis Island, 1904*

# The Story of Nicholas Gerros

*By modern standards, many people in
southeastern Europe were extremely poor around
1900. In Greece, which was ruled by Turkey
in those days, men had to find work in other
countries and return home briefly whenever
they could. Often they would send money for
one son to come to America in search of a better
life. Such is the story of Nicholas Gerros, as he
remembered it at age ninety:*

...When I went to get my passport I
walked down the mountain to this Kastoria
place. It was the first time I saw a wagon with
wheels. Six of us kids, all about fourteen, spent
a week in a big military building in Naples,
then two weeks a bit seasick till we unloaded
at Castle Garden and got the eye exam.

Some man came along. He gave us a box
of food. We had a ticket on us because we
couldn't speak English. They'd look at you and
tell you, you go there, or you go there.
Traveling was easy because it was prearranged
by the agents. We took a small boat from
New York to Norfolk, Virginia, and we were
waiting on the train and began to look in the
package to see what we had. Each of us had a
banana to go with the rest of the food that was
given him. We didn't know how to eat it. We'd

never seen bananas. Finally somebody realizes that on the train and showed us.

When we went to Cincinnati, there were some people there waiting for us. They showed us [how] to go direct to the apartment. When we got into this apartment they treated us with ice cream. It was the first time we all had ice cream. These people before us organized a room for us. There were more than a half-dozen rooms and a big kitchen.

I stayed with my father for a while, for all the while he was there. He was working in something concerning furniture. Just before the Balkan War started, he went back to Greece.

Those years there were no Greek woman coming to the United States. Mostly all the Greeks were young, between twelve and thirty. They had to kinda stick together because none of them knew any more of the English language than they did themselves.

I remember how hard—this you can put with a line under the words because they mean so much. The young people in America, they've got it so easy and they don't know how easy it is. I was asked to go out to buy something. I think I was in this country for two months. It was late spring. It was still cold, and I had to go down from the second floor. There were stairs going right straight down to the door. There was a bunch of young fellows there talking to each other and having a lot of fun. I was their age, but I couldn't speak any English.

I didn't want to get into any trouble with them so they're sitting down on the stairs and I tried to pass by to go do what I wanted to do. I didn't want to step on their clothes, so I was kind of careful and they realized that. One fellow, he wasn't sitting down, he was talking to a girl. I didn't know what he was saying. As far as I was concerned, any language was English to me, 'Let's have some fun with this fellow." So he came to me and talked, 'Blah blah." The first thing I know he gives me one upper cut and down I went.

Right in front of there was a bakery shop. This man is selling bread as well as cakes. He came out and the kids run away. He took me in. He asked me if I was hurt. Well, I [looked] and there was no blood so I says I wasn't hurt.

Right there and then I made up my mind. I'm going to school nights, learn the language, read, write, and spoken, and go to the YMCA to prepare myself to defend myself.

*Eventually, Nicholas Gerros moved to Haverhill, Massachusetts, where he worked in a shoe factory.*

*Eventually, he got his own clothing store. His advice? "You have to have a dream of what you want to be. You can find it. It will take time, like everything else takes time. The sooner you dream the better."*

# Just Draggin' Along Till The Freedom Come

*Catherine Moran McNamara was one of thousands of Irish women who immigrated here around 1900 and became domestic servants. Those from other countries looked down on this labor, but the potato famines and harsh conditions of farming had led many young girls into household service in Ireland. Furthermore, the Irish women's high literacy rate helped them adjust to city life in America. In her interview, at age ninety~three, Catherine remembers life in the "Old Country" and the changes she found in Massachusetts.*

In Ireland, we had to pay every cent we possibly could produce to taxes...My mother kept house and my father had no work but just the bit of land we had...Then if the year was bad and the stuff didn't grow, we suffered on that.

I've seen a family thrown out. I recall that distinctly because we took them in our barn. They had no place for their bed, for anything. I seen the little child, this is God's truth, I'll never forget this, it was just about a year and a half, put out on the little cradle...They had nothing, hadn't a cow. Everything they had was sold trying to pay the rent. The landlord, he was English, and the English owned Ireland then. They wouldn't let you go to church or nothing. You'd be jailed and shot dead one at a time....

Of course the ordinary people in England couldn't help that. There's some very nice people, decent English people, and there's some good people to work for. This is the government, they're like God you know. That's the way they are—with the kings and sirs and all. That's all folly, vanity, of the most foolish degree. That had to be *upheld* in Ireland. They had to take their hats off, and any Irishman wouldn't do it, they'd be jailed...

This was goin' down six hundred years— imagine being under anyone's thumb for that length of time! Just draggin' along till the freedom come. But one consolation, when America opened up. It took an awful lot of needy people here, and it opened a gap for them.

I came in at East Boston, stayed with my sister, started as a cook, and then went to the paper napkin factory in Framingham. $5.00 a week just to press your foot, cut the napkins, count out a dozen for each roll, and roll it up. A nice job.

I ended up doing housework, married a boilermaker in Lowell. He worked six days and after church Sundays. They didn't want us for the high jobs so they put out signs: NO IRISH NEED APPLY.

You have to go a long road before you'll be turnin' somewhere. We had six kids. The daughters became dressmakers, my son was a fireman. Another gave a lot to charity. "When a Protestant child is hungry,' he says, 'they are hungry as a Catholic child."

✳ ✳ ✳

## The Emigrant's Farewell

Farewell to thee, Ireland the land of our birth
The pride and the glory, the gem of the earth
We sail with sad hearts to a land far away
In search of that bread they may fail if we stay
New faces glow bright in the blaze of our fires
And the Saxon abides in the halls of our sires
Farewell, oh farewell to thy beautiful shore:
'Tis with tears that we bid thee farewell evermore.

*Source: Song adapted from an earlier song about leaving England, H.S. Thompson, 1885, published by W.A. Evans & Bro., 1885, Library of Congress, Music Division.*

# The Emigration of Rosa Cristofaro, 1884

*In Italy, many families saw marriage as the only way out of poverty for their daughters. When Rosa Cristofaro was fifteen and working in the silk mill, her true love had to leave for three years of military service. Mamma Lena decided that Rosa must marry, so when a neighbor named Santino offered to pay for her dress and had some gold as well, the marriage was arranged. When she was expecting their first child, her husband left for the United States:*

...one of those agents from the big bosses in America came to Bugiarno to get men for some iron mines in Missouri. The company paid for the tickets, but the men had to work for about a year to pay them back, and they had to work another year before they could send for their wives and families. So this time when that agent came Santino and some of his friends joined the gang and went off to America. He didn't even come back to the *osteria* to get his clothes.

When I heard that Santino was gone, oh, I was happy! I was thinking that probably I would never see that man again. America was a long way off...

*Rosa was happy that Santino had gone away. She enjoyed raising her son, Francesco, and had no desire to join her husband in America.*

My Francesco had learned to walk and was learning to talk when here, coming into the *osteria* one Sunday, were some of those men who had gone to America with Santino. I stopped playing with my baby and went and called Mamma Lena from the wine cellar.

"Those men in the iron mines in Missouri need women to do the cooking and washing," said one of the men. "Three men have sent back for their wives and, two for some girls to marry. Santino says for you to send Rosa. He sent the money and the ticket." And the man pulled them from an inside pocket and laid them on the table....

When the men were ready to leave the one who had brought the message spoke again. "In two weeks another gang of men from the villages is leaving for the iron mines in Missouri. Your daughter and the other wives and girls can go with them."...

"Yes, Rosa," she [Mamma Lena] said. "You must go....It would be a sin against God not to obey. You must go. But not Francesco. He didn't ask for Francesco and I would be too lonesome without him."...

Mamma Lena was good to me though. She thought I would be not so lonesome—not so homesick in America—if I had the oil like the poor always had in Bugiarno. So she made me three bottles full and sealed it up so it looked like wine. That oil is made from the seed of the mustard plant...Only the rich people in the cities in Italy can have the olive oil. We poor people used that oil that the women made themselves.

And so I had to leave Mamma Lena and my baby and go—off with that gang of men and one or two women to America.

The day came when we had to go and everyone was in the square saying good-bye. I had my Francesco in my arms. I was kissing his lips and kissing his cheeks and kissing his eyes. Maybe I would never see him again!...

"But Rosa, don't be so sad!...It is wonderful to go to America even if you don't want to go to Santino. You will get smart in America. And in America you will not be so poor."

Then Paris and we were being crowded into a train for Havre. We were so crowded we couldn't move, but my *paesani* were just laughing. "Who cares?" they laughed. "On our way to America! On our way to be millionaires!"

Day after day in Havre we were leaving the lodging house and standing down on the docks waiting for a ship to take us. But always the ship was full before it came our turn....

But here, on the sixth day we came on. We were almost the last ones. There was just one young French girl after us. She was with her mother and her sister, but when the mother and sister tried to follow, that *marinaro* at the gate said, "No more! Come on the next boat!" And that poor family was screaming and crying. But the *marinaro* wouldn't let the girl off and wouldn't let the mother and sister on. He said, "You'll meet in New York. Meet in New York."

All us poor people had to go down through a hole to the bottom of the ship. There was a big dark room down there with rows of wooden shelves all around where we were going to sleep—the Italian, the German, the Polish, the Swede, the French—every kind. And in that time the third class on the boat was not like now. The girls and women and the men had to sleep all together in the same room. The men and girls had to sleep even in the same bed with only those little half-boards up between to keep us from rolling together. But I was lucky. I had two girls sleeping next to me. When the dinner bell rang we were all standing in line holding the tin plates we had to buy in Havre, waiting for soup and bread.

"Oh, I'm so scared!" Emilia kept saying and she kept looking at the little picture she carried in her blouse. "I'm so scared!"

"Don't be scared, Emilia." I told her. "That young man looks nice in his picture."

"But I don't know him." she said. "I was only seven years old when he went away."...

On the fourth day a terrible storm came. The sky grew black and the ocean came over the deck. Sailors started running everywhere, fastening this and fastening that and giving orders. Us poor people had to go below and that little door to the deck was fastened down. We had no light and no air and everyone got sick where we were....

About two hours later me and my *paesani* were back at Castle Garden on a government boat...I wanted to hold onto my bottles of oil—they might get broken—but the officers made me leave those too. Then one by one we went through a narrow door into Castle Garden. The inside was a big, dark room full of dust, with fingers of light coming down from the ceiling. That room was already crowded with poor people from earlier boats sitting on benches and on railings and on the floor. And to one side were a few old tables where food was being sold. Down the center between two railings high-up men were sitting on stools at high desks. And we had to walk in line between those two railings and pass them.

Every new arrival at Ellis Island went through a medical exam and an eye test (c. 1913)

"What is your name? Where do you come from? Where are you going?"

Those men knew all the languages and could tell just by looking what country we come from....

"Cristoforo, Rosa. From Lombardy. To the iron mine in Missouri."...

"Get your baggage and come back. Wait by the visitors' door—there at the left. Your name will be called. All right. Move on!"

There were two other desks—one for railroad tickets and one for American money—but we *Lombardi* had ours already so we went back for our bundles. But I couldn't find my straw-covered bottles. Everybody was trying to help me find them. Then an inspector man came. "What's all the commotion?" he asked. "Oh, so those bottles belonged to her? Well ask her," he said to the interpreter. "Ask her what that stuff was? Was it poison?"

When Pep told him he said, "Well tell her her bottles are in the bottom of the ocean! Tell her that's what she gets for bringing such nasty stuff into America! It made us all sick!"

My *paesani* looked at their feet or at the ground and hurried back into the building. Then they busted out laughing. That was a good one!...I was brokenhearted to lose my good oil but it was funny anyway—how Mamma Lena's nice wine bottles had fooled those men in gold braid.

We *Lombardi* put down our bundles and sat on the floor near the visitors' door. At last after all the new immigrants had been checked, an officer at the door started calling the names. "Gruffiano, Emilia" was the first one.

*"Presente! Presente!"* shouted Pep jumping to his feet and waving his hands. But Emilia was so scared I had to pull her up and drag her along after him.

At the door the officer called the name again and let us pass. Then here came up a young man. He was dressed—O Madonna!—like the president of the United States! White gloves and a cane and a diamond pin in his tie. Emilia tried to run away but Pep pulled her back. *"Non è vero! Non è vero!* It's not true!" she kept saying.

"But it is true!" the young man laughed. "Look at me, Emilia! Don't you remember Carlo who used to play the *tromba* in San Paola when you were a little girl?" And he pulled her out from behind us and took her in his arms and kissed her. (In America a man can kiss the girl he is going to marry!) "But I never thought you would come like this," he said, holding her off a little and looking at her headkerchief and full skirt. "I'm afraid to look. Did you come in the wooden soles too?"

"No," said Emilia, speaking to him for the first time.

"My mother bought me real shoes to come to America!" And she was lifting her feet to show him.

"She looks just the same as when she was seven years old," the young man said to Pep, and he was happy and laughing. "But I'm going to take her up Broad Street and buy her some American clothes before I take her home."...

When the gate was opened men wearing badges came running in, going to the different people. One dressed-up man with a cane and waxed mustache came to us. *"Buongiorno, paesani! Benvenuto!* Welcome to America! Welcome to the new country!" He was speaking Italian and English too and putting out his hand to shake hands with Pep. We other *paesani* looked on in wonder. A high man like that shaking hands with the poor! This was America for sure!

"My dear man," laughed Bartini, "you're lucky I found you. There's no train to Missouri for three days. But don't worry! Bartini will take care of everything. You can come and eat and sleep in my hotel, comfortable and nice, and in three days I will take you and put you on the right train."

And in three days he did put us on the train but he took all our money first, about thirteen dollars each one. He left us not even a crust of bread for our journey. And we didn't even guess that he was fooling us.

The American people on the train were sorry when they saw we had nothing to eat and they were trying to give us some of their food. But Pep said no. He was too proud to take it....Those American people were dressed up nice—the ladies had hats and everything—but they were riding the same class with us poor—all equal and free together....

Then the conductor was calling, "Union! Union!"

And everybody was picking up bundles and pushing to the windows. There was a little wooden station ahead and beside it were all our *paesani* from the iron mine with two wagons with horses to meet us....

I thought maybe Santino didn't come, or maybe I'd forgotten what he looked like. But then I saw him—a little back from the others—just as I remembered him....

It was like a *festa*. Everybody in their best clothes and everybody talking and laughing....

"Watch close the way we are going, Rosa." It was Gionin...He was sitting next to me on the wagon. "You will be walking back here every two or three days to get groceries and ask for mail." He was not *Lombardo* like the others—he and his friend were *Toscani*. I had to listen careful to understand his words...

"Here in America they have the courthouse and the jail on the square, in place of a church.".…

After two or three miles the wagons came out from the woods and there, below, was the iron mine and the camp. Down there there were no trees and no grass—just some shacks made of boards and some railroad tracks. The sun was going down behind the hills and a few miners with picks and sledgehammers were coming out from a tunnel. Other men down in an open place were wheeling away their tools in wheelbarrows. The new *paesani* grew silent—as if they had expected something else—as if they were no longer sure they were going to be millionaires. And me, looking up to see which shack Gionin was pointing to, met the eyes of Santino.

✷

# I Thought I Heard My Mother, by Rose Romano

We came to this country to get away
from suffering, not to bring it with us.
Why should we tell the children? Why
would we want the children to
know suffering? I thought I heard my
mother say she lived in a cave back in
Sicily, slept next to a mule which
the family was proud to own. She
never told me about it. Why should
we tell the children?

My son speaks English with an
American accent, doesn't speak a word
of Italian. He has a good job, a nice
home, an American wife. Nobody
bothers them since he changed his
name. Why should the children know
suffering?

Inside he's still a good Italian boy.
He visits my mother on Sundays. When
he calls her Grandmother, he
makes it sound like a royal title.
He knows how to show respect. When
he was a little boy

He called her Nonna. Sometimes
I miss that little boy. He has a
son who calls me Grammy, but
it's not the same.

# Excerpts from *The Independent*

*The following excerpts were narrated to reporters of* The Independent *in New York City at the beginning of the twentieth century. The editor wanted unknown and undistinguished Americans to have the chance to share their lives and their stories. Like each person who has come to America, the stories are unique in many ways, yet they share a comman thread.*

## From an Italian immigrant

...We came to Brooklyn, New York, to a wooden house in Adams street that was full of Italians from Naples. Bartolo had a room on the third floor and there were fifteen men in the room, all boarding with Bartolo. He did the cooking on a stove in the middle of the room and there were beds all around the sides, one bed above another. It was very hot in the room, but we were soon asleep, for we were very tired.

The next morning, early, Bartolo told us to got out and pick rags and get bottles. He gave us bags and hooks and showed us the ash barrels. On the streets where the fine houses are the people are very careless and put out good things, like mattresses and umbrellas, clothes, bats and boots. We brought all these to Bartolo and he made them new again and sold them on the sidewalk; but mostly we brought rags and bones. The rags we had to wash in the back yard and then we hung them to dry on lines under the ceiling in our room. The bones we kept under the beds till Bartolo could find a man to buy them.

Most of the men in our room worked at digging the sewer. Bartolo got them the work and they paid him about one-quarter of their wages. Then he charged them for board and he bought the clothes for them, too. So they got little money after all.

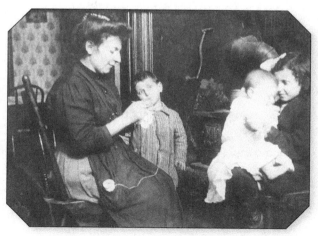

*Italian immigrant family, learning lacemaking (Lewis Hine, 1911)*

Bartolo was always saying that the rent of the room was so high that he could not make anything, but he was really making plenty. He was what they call a padrone and is now a very rich man.

## A Hungarian arrives in New York Harbor

...A well dressed man who spoke our language told us that the big iron woman in the harbor was a goddess that gave out liberty freely and without cost to everybody. He said the thing in her hand that looked like a broom was light—that it was to give us light and liberty too...he told us a man could stand inside the broom....

## A Swede buys a farm near Minneapolis

...I and my sister Helene came to this country together in 1899, Hilda having sent us the money, 600 kroner. We came over in the steerage from Gothenburg, on the west coast. The voyage wasn't bad. They give people beds in the steerage now, and all their food, and it is very good and well cooked. It took us twelve days to cross the sea, but we did not feel it long, as when people got over the seasickness there was plenty of dancing, for most of the people in the steerage were Swedes and very pleasant and friendly. On fine days we could walk outside on the deck. Two men had concertinas and one had a violin....

I worked for my brother from August 1899, to March, 1901, at $10 a month, making $304, of which I spent only $12 in that time, as I had clothes.

On the first day of March I went to a farm that I had bought for $150, paying $50 down. It was a bush farm, ten miles from my brother's place and seven miles from the nearest cross roads store. A man had owned it and cleared two acres, and then fallen sick and the storekeeper got it for a debt and sold it to me. My brother heard of it and advised me to buy it.

I went on this land in company with a French Canadian named Joachim. He was part Indian, and yet was laughing all the time, very gay, very full of fun, and yet the best axman I ever saw. He wore the red trimmed white blanket overcoat of the Hudson Bay Company, with white blanket trousers and fancy moccasins, and a red sash around his waist and a capote that went over his head.

# A Lithuanian finds work

...[In Lithuania you paid] with sacks of
rye. But here you want a hundred things.
Whenever you walk out you see new things
you want, and you must have money to buy
everything....

The next morning my friends woke me at
five o'clock and said, "Now, if you want life,
liberty and happiness," they laughed, "you
must push for yourself. You must get a job.
Come with us!' And we went to the [Chicago
stock] yards. Men and women were walking in
by thousands as far as we could see. We went
to the doors of one big slaughter house. There
was a crowd of about 200 men waiting there
for a job. They looked hungry and kept
watching the door. At last a special policeman
came out and began pointing to men, one by
one. Each one jumped forward. Twenty-three
were taken. Then they all went inside, and all
the others turned their faces away and looked
tired. I remember one boy sat down and cried,
just next to me, on a pile of boards. Some
policemen waved their clubs and we all walked
on. I found some Lithuanians to talk with,
who told me they had come every morning for
three weeks. Soon we met other crowds
coming away from other slaughter houses, and

we all walked around and felt bad and tired and hungry.

That night I told my friends that I would not do this many days, but would go some place else. "Where?" they asked me, and I began to see then that I was in bad trouble, because I spoke no English. Then one man told me to give him $5 to give the special policeman. I did this and the next morning the policeman pointed me out, so I had a job....

The union is doing another good thing. It is combining all the nationalities. The night I joined the Cattle Butchers' Union I was led into the room by a negro member. With me were Bohemians, Germans and Poles, and Mike Donnelly, the President, is an Irishman....

## A Jewish immigrant from Poland

...When I was a little more than ten years of age my father died....We needed little, it is true, but even soup, black bread and onions we could not always get.

We struggled along till I was nearly thirteen years of age and quite handy at housework and shop-keeping, so far as I could learn them there. But we fell behind in the rent and mother kept thinking more and more that we should have to leave Poland and go across the sea to America where we heard it was much easier to make money. Mother wrote to Aunt Fanny, who lived in New York, and told her how hard it was to live In Poland, and Aunt Fanny advised her to come and bring me. I was out at service at this time and mother thought she would leave me—as I had a good place—and come to this country alone, sending for me afterward. But Aunt Fanny would not hear of this. She said we should both come at once, and she went around among our relatives in New York and took up a subscription for our passage.

We came by steerage on a steamship in a very dark place that smelt dreadfully. There were hundreds of other people packed in with us, men, women and children, and almost all of them were sick. It took us twelve days to cross the sea, and we thought we should die, but at last the voyage was over, and we came up and saw the beautiful bay and the big woman with the spikes on her head and the lamp that is lighted at night In her hand (Goddess of Liberty).

Aunt Fanny and her husband met us at the gate of this country and were very good to us, and soon I had a place to live out (domestic servant), while my mother got work in a factory making white goods....

But mother had a very gay disposition. She liked to go around and see everything, and friends took her about New York at night and she caught a bad cold and coughed and coughed. She really had hasty consumption, but she didn't know it, and I didn't know it, and she tried to keep on working, but it was no use. She had not the strength. Two doctors attended her, but they could do nothing, and at last she died and I was left alone.

I had saved money while out at service, but mother's sickness and funeral swept it all away and now I had to begin all over again.

Aunt Fanny had always been anxious for me to get an education, as I did not know how to read or write, and she thought that was wrong. Schools are different in Poland from what they are in this country, and I was always too busy to learn to read and write. So when mother died I thought I would try to learn a trade and then I could go to school at night and learn to speak the English language well.

So I went to work in Allen Street (Manhattan) in what they call a sweatshop, making skirts by machine. I was new at the work and the foreman scolded me a great deal....

I did not know at first that you must not look around and talk, and I made many mistakes with the sewing, so that I was often called a "stupid animal." But I made $4 a week by working six days in the week. For there are two Sabbaths here—our own Sabbath, that comes on a Saturday, and the Christian Sabbath that comes on Sunday. It is against our law to work on our own Sabbath, so we work on their Sabbath.

*Polish immigrant family working on a Maryland farm (Lewis Hine, 1909)*

# Freedom of expression for a Syrian in New York in 1898

...As I advanced in school I was taught penmanship. This is a most important accomplishment in Syria. When one says that a certain person is a penman it means much; it means that he is a scholar in the eyes of the community. Good penmen are much respected.

...It was about fifteen years ago when I first began to attend the American mission school. This was very different from that which was taught by the friar. At the first school there were few books and I got the impression that there were only about 500 different books in the world, the most important being the Syrian Bible and some writings of our saints....

There was an enclyclopedia at the American school which I learned how to use after a time and this broadened my ideas. I read the articles on Syria and the United States, and found to my astonishment that the book made the United States out to be a far larger and richer country than Syria or even Turkey....

One time a boy of about my own age told me that if I went up the mountains a mile and a half and looked under the exposed roots of a great tree to which he pointed I would find something good. He was a bold, wild boy and I did not know what he meant or whether he was just joking. Nevertheless I went as he directed and in a copper cylinder I found a number of newspapers which were printed in Arabic. They were from New York, written by Syrians residing there, and they bitterly attacked the Government of Lebanon, the Maronite priests and the Sultan of Turkey, saying that Lebanon and Syria could never have freedom till all these were overthrown.

I was much frightened at reading these papers and quickly put them back where I had found them and ran away from the place, for I thought that if any priest found me with them I might lose my life....

Little by little my mind began to change and my eyes to open, till I could see that our people really were suffering terrible wrongs which did not exist in some other countries....

[Then my uncle] went to Beirut and asked about the steamships there, and we found that we could get one that would take us direct to New York....

My uncle had a friend who met us at Ellis Island and helped to get us quickly out of the vessel, and ten hours after we had come into the bay we were established in two rooms in the third story of a brick house in Washington Street, only three blocks away from Battery Park. Two minutes' walk from us was roaring Broadway,....

I went at night also and saw the city more wonderful than ever, the buildings outlined in the darkness, in chains and rows and circles and ropes of various colored lights—illuminated diamonds and rubies, emeralds, pearl topazes and all other gems. Never was there such an illumination.

I had learned English in the mission school and as I was a good penman I had no difficulty in securing work as a clerk in an Oriental goods store, where some other Syrians were employed. My uncle, who understands the art of inlaying with silver, ivory and mother of pearl, also got work, and my mother kept house for us and added to our joint income by embroidering slippers after the Lebanon fashion. Between us we earned $22 a week, and as our rent was only $10 a month and food did not cost any more than $6 a week, we saved money....later [I] started a printing office of my own in Washington Street, which is the center of our quarter. Soon I had a newspaper of my own. This now comes out three times a week.

# Excerpts from *A Bintel Brief*

*A great many of the 2,650,000 Jews who immigrated to America from Eastern European countries between 1881 and 1925 settled in the old tenements of the Lower East Side in New York City. Tales of this Golden Land turned into hard necessities of breaking tradition and of "sweatshop" conditions or unemployment.*

*Some pushcart peddlers sold eyeglasses and kept a mirror on a stick. Others sold horse radish and padlocked their churning machines to a lamppost. Skilled tailors and young children worked long hours and gradually created the garment district. Everyone worked for better labor conditions. A Yiddish daily newspaper begun in 1897 gave a a voice to their protests and to their perseverance. What follows are some of their outcries, printed in "A Bintel Brief" (Bundle of Letters), a feature of the* Jewish Daily Forward.

## 1907

Worthy Editor,

I am eighteen years old and a machinist by trade. During the past year I suffered a great deal, just because I am a Jew.

It is common knowledge that my trade is run mainly by the Gentiles and, working among the Gentiles, I have seen things that cast a dark shadow on the American labor scene. Just listen:

I worked in a shop in a small town in New Jersey, with twenty Gentiles. There was one other Jew besides me, and both of us endured the greatest hardships. That we were insulted goes without saying. At times we were even beaten up. We work in an area where there are many factories, and once, when we were leaving the shop, a group of workers fell on us like hoodlums and beat us. To top it off, we and one of our attackers were arrested. The hoodlum was let out on bail, but we, beaten and bleeding, had to stay in jail. At the trial, they fined the hoodlum eight dollars and let him go free.

After that I went to work on a job in Brooklyn. As soon as they found out that I was a Jew they began to torment me so that I had to leave the place. I have already worked at many places, and I either have to leave, voluntarily, or they fire me because I am a Jew.

Till now, I was alone and didn't care. At this trade you can make good wages, and I had enough. But now I've brought my parents over, and of course I have to support them.

Lately I've been working on one job for three months and I would be satisfied, but the worm of anti-Semitism is beginning to eat at my bones again. I go to work in the morning as to Gehenna, and I run away at night as from a fire. It's impossible to talk to them because they are common boors, so-called "American sports." I have already tried in various ways, but the only way to deal with them is with a strong fist. But I am too weak and they are too many.

Perhaps you can help me in this matter. I know it is not an easy problem.

Your reader,
E.H.

Answer:

In the answer, the Jewish machinist is advised to appeal to the United Hebrew Trades and ask them to intercede for him and bring up charges before the Machinists Union about this persecution. His attention is also drawn to the fact that there are Gentile factories where Jews and Gentiles work together and get along well with each other.

Finally it is noted that people will have to work long and hard before this senseless racial hatred can be completely uprooted.

*Many immigrants lived in densely-packed tenement buildings upon their arrival in American cities*

## 1908

My dearest friend of the *Forward*,

I appeal to you for help, since I have no better comrades than the workers.

I have been jobless for six months now. I have eaten the last shirt on my back and now there is nothing left for me but to end my life. I have struggled long enough in the dark world. Death is better than such a life. One goes about with strong hands, one wants to sell them for a bit of bread, and no one wants to buy. They tell you cold-bloodedly: "We don't need you." Can you imagine how heartsick one gets?

I get up at four in the morning to hunt a job through the newspaper. I have no money for carfare, so I go on foot, but by the time I get to the place there are hundreds before me. Then I run wherever my eyes lead me. Lately I've spent five cents a day on food, and the last two days I don't have even that. I have no strength to go on.

I am an ironworker. I can work a milling machine and a drill press. I can also drive horses and train colts. In Russia I served in the cavalry, and there I once hit my superior. For that I was sent to prison for forty days. Then I was returned to my squadron and my case was transferred to the military court in Kiev. Then orders came for me to be brought to Kiev.

When I learned of this I fled at three o'clock in the morning. I gave my gun and sword to the Bund organization and they gave me passage money to America.

If I had known it would be so bitter for me here, I wouldn't have come. I didn't come here for a fortune, but where is bread? What can I do now? I ask you, comrades. I beg you to help me in my dire need. Do not let a man die a horrible death.

Your friend,
G.B.

# 1911

Dear Editor,

I am a newsboy, fourteen years old, and I sell the *Forverts* [the *Jewish Daily Forward*] in the streets till late into the night. I come to you to ask your advice.

I was born in Russia and was twelve years old when I came to America with my dear mother. My sister, who was in the country before us, brought us over.

My sister worked and supported us. She didn't allow me to go to work but sent me to school. I went to school for two years and didn't miss a day, but then came the terrible fire at the Triangle shop, where she worked, and I lost my dear sister. My mother and I suffer terribly from the misfortune. I had to help my mother and after school hours I go out and sell newspapers.

I have to go to school three more years, and after that I want to go to college. But my mother doesn't want me to go to school because she thinks I should go to work. I tell her that I will work days and study at night but she won't hear of it.

Since I read the *Forverts* to my mother every night and read your answers in the "Bintel Brief," I beg you to answer me and say a few words to her.

Your Reader,
The Newsboy

# The Joy of Growing Up Italian

*The following is an essay from an anonymous contemporary "American Italian."*

I was well into adulthood before I realized that I was an American. Of course, I had been born in America and had lived here all of my life, but somehow it never occurred to me that just being a citizen of the United States meant I was an American. Americans were people who ate peanut butter and jelly on mushy white bread that came out of plastic packages, while I ate peppers and egg sandwiches on an Italian roll. I was Italian.

For me, as I am sure for most second generation Italian-American children who grew up in the 40s and 50s, there was a definite distinction between US and THEM. We were Italian. Everybody else—the Irish, German, Polish, Jewish, etc.—they were the "MED-E-GONES." [Americans] There was no animosity involved in that distinction no prejudice, no hard feelings, just—well—we were sure ours was the better way. For instance, we had a bread man, a milk man, a coal and ice man, a fruit and vegetable man, a watermelon man, an egg and cheese man, and a fish man; we even had a man who sharpened knives and scissors who came right to our homes, or at least right outside our homes. They were the many peddlers who plied the Italian neighborhoods. We would wait for their call, their yell, their individual sound. We knew them all and they knew us. Americans went to the stores for most of their foods. What a waste!

...Sunday was truly the big day of the week. That was the day you would wake up to the smell of garlic and onions frying in olive oil. As you laid in bed, you could hear the hiss as tomatoes were dropped into a pan. Sundays we always had gravy (the MED-E-GONES called it SAUCE) and macaroni (they called it PASTA). Sunday would not be Sunday without going to Mass. Of course, you could not eat before Mass because you had to fast before receiving Communion. But the good part was we knew when we got home we would find hot meatballs frying and nothing tastes better than newly fried meatballs and crisp bread dipped into the pot of gravy.

There was another difference between US and THEM. We had gardens; not just flower gardens, but huge gardens where we grew tomatoes, tomatoes and more tomatoes. We ate them, cooked them, jarred them. Of course, we also grew peppers, basil, lettuce and squash. Everybody had a grapevine and a fig tree and in the fall, everybody made homemade wine, lots of it. Of course these gardens thrived so because we also had something else it seemed our American friends didn't have. We had a GRANDFATHER!! It's not that they didn't have grandfathers, it's just that they didn't live in the same house or on the same block. They visited their grandfathers. We ate with ours, and God forbid we didn't see him at least once a day. I can still remember my Grandfather telling me about how he came to America as a young man, "on the boat." How the family lived in rented apartments or small houses and took in boarders in order to make ends meet, how he decided he didn't want his children, five sons and two daughters, to grow up in that environment. All of this, of course, in his own version of Italian/English which I soon learned to understand quite well.

So, when he saved enough, and I could never figure out how, he bought a house. That house served as the family headquarters for the next 10 years. I remember when he would have to leave, he would rather sit on the back porch and watch his garden grow and when he would leave for some special occasion, he had to return as quickly as possible. After all "nobody's watching the house."

I also remember the holidays when all the relatives would gather at my Grandfather's house and there would be tables full of food and homemade wine and music. Women in the kitchen, men in the living room and kids, kids everywhere. I must have a half million cousins, first and second and some who aren't even related, but what did it matter. And my Grandfather, cigar in his mouth and his fine trimmed mustache, would sit in the middle of it all grinning his mischievous smile, his dark eyes twinkling, surveying his domain, proud of his family and how well his children had done. One was a barber, one had his father's trade, one was a policeman, of course, there was always the rogue. And the girls, they had all married well and had fine husbands and healthy children and everyone knew respect.

He had achieved his goal of coming to America and to Philadelphia and how his children and their children were achieving the same goals that were available to them in this great Country because they were Americans. When my Grandfather died years ago at the age of 76 things began to change. Slowly at first, but then Uncles and Aunts eventually began to cut down on their visits. Family gatherings were fewer and something seemed to be missing, although when we did get together, usually at my mother's house now, I always had the feeling he was there somehow. It was understandable of course. Everyone had their own families now and their own grandchildren. Today they visit once or twice a year. Today we meet at weddings and wakes.

Lots of other things have changed too. The old house my Grandfather bought is now covered with aluminum siding, although my uncle still lives there, and of course my Grandfather's garden is gone. The last of the homemade wine has long since been drunk and nobody covers the fig tree in the fall anymore. For a while we would make the rounds on the Holidays visiting family. Now we occasionally visit the cemetery. A lot of them are there, Grandparents, Aunts, Uncles, even my own father.

The holidays have changed too. The great quantity of food we once consumed without any ill effects is not good for us anymore. Too much starch, too much cholesterol, too many calories and nobody bothers to bake anymore—too busy—and it's easier to buy it now and too much is no good for you. We meet at my house now, at least my family does, but it's not the same.

The difference between US and THEM are not so easily defined anymore and I guess that's good. My grandparents were Italian Italians, my parents were Italian Americans, and I'm an American Italian and my children are American Americans. Oh, I'm an American alright and proud of it, just as my grandfather would want me to be. We are all Americans now—Irish, German, Poles, Jews, etc., U.S. Citizens all—but somehow I still feel ITALIAN. All I do know is that my children have been created out of a wonderful piece of the heritage.

They never knew my grandfather.

# Definitions

gendarme – a member of the French police, part of the armed forces serving as frontier and customs guards.

mujik – a peasant in Czarist Russia

padrone – a man who exploits Italian immigrants in America; a master, owner, or manager.

paesani – Italian peasants; kindred people

ruse – an action meant to confuse or mislead

verst – a Russian measure of distance, equivalent to two-thirds of a mile.

## Note

Castle Garden: Originally a fort at the foot of Manhattan, near Battery Park, Castle Garden was converted to use as the first formal receiving station for immigrants anywhere in the world. Steerage class immigrants arriving in New York from 1855 to 1892 were processed there. First and second class passengers were able to disembark at Staten Island.

Steerage class travellers received their medical exams could exchange foreign currency for U.S. currency, and could purchase land travel tickets at Castle Garden. There was also an employment agency on the grounds, which enabled some to find jobs upon their arrival.

After 1892, Ellis Island became the location for medical exams and interviews for newly arrived immigrants.

# Bibliography

Antin, Mary, *From Plotzsk to Boston,* Boston: W. B. Clarke, 1899.

___, *The Promised Land,* Boston: Houghton Mifflin, 1911.

Brownstone, David M., Irene M. Franck, Douglass L. Brownstone, *Island of Hope, Island of Tears,* New York: Rawson, Wade, 1979.

Ets, Marie Hall, *Rosa: The Life of an Italian Immigrant,* Minneapolis: University of Minneapolis Press, 1970.

Fisher, L. E., *Ellis Island: Gateway to the New World,* New York: Holiday House, 1986.

Handlin, Oscar, *The Uprooted: the Epic Story of the Great Migrations that Made the American People,* Boston: Little, Brown, 1973 (2nd ed.).

Holt, Hamilton, *Life Stories of Undistinguished Americans, As Told By Themselves,* New York: James Pott, 1906.

Jones, Maldwyn Allen, *American Immigration,* Chicago History of American Civilization, Chicago: Chicago U. P., 1960.

Metzker, Isaac, ed., *A Bintel Brief: Sixty Years of Letters from the Lower East Side to the Jewish Daily Forward,* New York: Ballantine Books, 1972.

Namias, June, *First Generation: In the Words of Twentieth Century American Immigrants,* Boston: Beacon Press, 1978.

Steiner, Dale, *Of Thee We Sing: Immigrants and American History,* Orlando: Harcourt, Brace, Jovanovich, 1987.
Films: *Molly's Pilgrim*

CPSIA information can be obtained
at www.ICGtesting.com
Printed in the USA
BVHW070815101218
535223BV00029B/928